A Special Gift

PRESENTED TO:

FROM:

DATE:

Reflections

FROM A MOTHER'S HEART

A FAMILY LEGACY FOR YOUR CHILDREN

YOUR LIFE STORY IN YOUR OWN WORDS

CONTENTS

*D*ays pass…seasons change…
months meld into years, and we stand
looking back at our lives—childhood
memories, exciting moments, crises, and
turning points.

In January we think of new beginnings;
in February of valentines, first dates,
and first kisses. Does ever a June pass
without thoughts of our own wedding
day? Surely summer evokes backseat
memories of seemingly unending trips
to grandma's house or the beach. And
don't November and December bring to
mind family traditions and celebrations
held tightly through the years?

Like ivy on the garden trellis, our
lives are inescapably entwined with the
seasons and months of the year. That is
why we have designed this mother's
memory journal in a twelve-month

format. Each month features twelve intriguing questions with space to write a personal answer. Questions explore family history, childhood memories, lighthearted incidents, cherished traditions, and the dreams and spiritual adventures encountered in a lifetime of living.

Whether you choose to complete the journal in a few days, weeks, or over the course of a year, the questions will take you on a journey through the times and seasons of your life. This makes a tangible family record to pass on as a gift to a son or daughter, a loving memoir of written words that are windows to a mother's heart.

No matter what your age, memory and reminiscence open a richer, fuller understanding of who you are as a family. Let this memory journal be a starting point—a door into discussing and sharing the unique qualities of your life. May *Reflections from a Mother's Heart* draw you closer to each other as you share the experiences of a lifetime.

PERSONAL PORTRAIT

your full given name _____

your date of birth _____

your place of birth _____

your mother's full name _____

the place and date of her birth _____

your father's full name _____

the place and date of his birth _____

the names of your paternal grandparents _____

the places and dates of their births _____

the names of your maternal grandparents _____

the places and dates of their births _____

the names of your siblings _____

the places and dates of their births _____

_____

_____

the date and place of your marriage _____

the full given name of your husband _____

the names and birth dates of your children _____

_____

_____

WHAT IS YOUR FAVORITE?

flower _____ Bible verse _____

perfume _____ dessert _____

color _____ vacation spot _____

hymn or song _____ type of food _____

book _____ sport _____

author _____ leisure activity _____

January

The beauty
of the written word
is that it can be held
close to the heart
and read over
and over again.

• •

FLORENCE LITTAUER

What was your favorite pastime as a child?
Did you prefer doing it alone or with someone else?

*W*ho gave you your name and why? Did you have a family nickname? How did you get it?

Describe your childhood bedroom.
What was the view from your window?

*W*ere you baptized or dedicated as an infant?
If so, where and by whom?

*W*hen did you first go to church?
What are your earliest memories of church?

*W*here did your father go to
work every day and what did he do?

_____
_____
_____
_____
_____
_____
_____
_____
_____
_____
_____
_____
_____
_____
_____
_____
_____
_____
_____
_____
_____
_____
_____

*H*ow did your mother spend her day?
Did she have a job or do volunteer work outside the home?

*D*escribe what the family living room looked like when you were a child.

_____
_____
_____
_____
_____
_____
_____
_____
_____
_____
_____
_____
_____
_____
_____
_____
_____
_____
_____
_____
_____
_____
_____
_____

*W*hat kind of prayer did you say before you went to sleep? Who taught you how to pray it?

_____

_____

_____

_____

_____

_____

_____

_____

_____

_____

_____

_____

_____

_____

_____

_____

_____

_____

_____

_____

_____

$\mathcal{W}$here was your childhood home located?
Did you enjoy living there?

_____
_____
_____
_____
_____
_____
_____
_____
_____
_____
_____
_____
_____
_____
_____
_____
_____
_____
_____
_____
_____
_____

_D_escribe your grandparents' houses.
Did you visit them often? Why or why not?

*L*ist one special memory about each of your brothers and sisters.

_____
_____
_____
_____
_____

_____
_____
_____
_____
_____
_____
_____
_____
_____
_____
_____
_____
_____
_____
_____
_____

JANUARY

Recall for me some of the most important lessons you have learned in life:

_____
_____
_____
_____
_____
_____
_____
_____
_____
_____
_____
_____
_____
_____
_____
_____
_____
_____
_____
_____
_____
_____
_____
_____

February

For all of us,
today's experiences are
tomorrow's memories.

• • •

BARBARA JOHNSON

*S*hare a memory of your grandparents or an older person you loved.

Who was the first person to talk to you about God?
What effect did this have on you?

When did you become a Christian? How did your life change?

_____
_____
_____
_____
_____
_____
_____
_____
_____
_____
_____
_____
_____
_____
_____
_____
_____
_____
_____
_____
_____
_____
_____
_____
_____
_____
_____
_____

Who gave you your first Bible and how old were you when you received it? How did it influence your life?

*D*escribe a memorable Valentine you received.

How ow far did you have to travel to attend elementary, junior high, and high school, and how did you get there?

What scent or sound immediately takes you back to childhood? Describe the feeling it evokes.

_____
_____
_____
_____
_____
_____
_____
_____
_____
_____
_____
_____
_____
_____
_____
_____
_____
_____
_____
_____
_____
_____
_____
_____
_____
_____
_____

*W*hat was your favorite meal when you were a child?
What made it your favorite?

What was the name of your favorite pet?
Why was it your favorite?

_____
_____
_____
_____
_____
_____
_____
_____
_____
_____
_____
_____
_____
_____
_____
_____
_____
_____
_____
_____
_____
_____
_____
_____

What chores did you have to do when you were growing up? Did you get an allowance? How much was it?

$\mathcal{T}$ell me about your first job.

Share a story about a severe winter storm.

Share your favorite dessert recipe:

March

The mother's heart
is the child's schoolroom.

HENRY WARD BEECHER

Did the pastor or a visiting missionary ever come to your house for dinner or tea? Share one vivid experience.

_____

_____

_____

_____

_____

_____

_____

_____

_____

_____

_____

_____

_____

_____

_____

_____

_____

_____

_____

_____

_____

_____

_____

*D*id you ever feel that God had a special calling on your life?

When did you first start to pray? What do you remember about your early prayers?

_W_ho was your favorite teacher? Why?

*D*escribe one of your favorite dress-up outfits as a child.
On what occasions would you wear it?

_____

_____

_____

_____

_____

_____

_____

_____

_____

_____

_____

_____

_____

_____

_____

_____

_____

_____

_____

_____

*D*id you ever have a special
hideaway or playhouse?
What made it special?

*W*hat extracurricular activities were you involved in during high school? Why did you choose those activities?

_____

_____

_____

_____

_____

_____

_____

_____

_____

_____

_____

_____

_____

_____

_____

_____

_____

_____

_____

_____

_____

_____

What was the hardest thing you ever had to do?

*W*hat crazy fads do you remember in grade school?

*W*hen did you have your first date? Tell me about it.

*W*hat do you remember about your first kiss?

_____
_____
_____
_____
_____
_____
_____
_____
_____
_____
_____
_____
_____
_____
_____
_____
_____
_____
_____
_____
_____
_____
_____
_____
_____
_____

What did you do to celebrate birthdays when you were growing up?

_____
_____
_____
_____
_____
_____
_____
_____
_____
_____
_____
_____
_____
_____
_____
_____
_____
_____
_____
_____
_____
_____
_____

Record here some gardening or decorating tips
that you have found helpful:

_____

_____

_____

_____

_____

_____

_____

_____

_____

_____

_____

_____

_____

_____

_____

_____

_____

_____

_____

_____

_____

_____

April

However time or circumstance
may come between
a mother and her child,
their lives are
interwoven forever.

• • •

PAM BROWN

hat were some of the most memorable books
you read as a child? What made them memorable?

What were your family finances like when you were growing up? How did that affect you?

*D*o you remember your first communion? What influence did it have on you and your family?

What mischievous childhood experience do you remember? How did it affect you?

*W*hat meaningful advice did you receive from an adult? What were the circumstances?

As a teenager did you rebel or do things your parents wouldn't have approved of? How do you feel about that now?

APRIL

$\mathcal{W}$hen did you first learn about sex? What was your reaction?

What things do you wish you had done in childhood or adolescence?

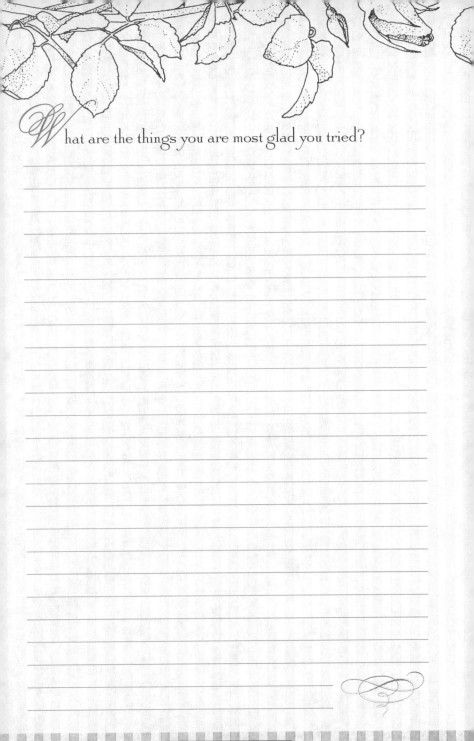

What are the things you are most glad you tried?

*D*escribe your mother in her best dress.

$\mathcal{D}$escribe your father in his working clothes.

What did your family like to do on weekends?
Describe one particularly memorable event.

_____

_____

_____

_____

_____

_____

_____

_____

_____

_____

_____

_____

_____

_____

_____

_____

_____

_____

_____

_____

_____

_____

Share one of your mother's best recipes or
a recipe for one of your favorite childhood dishes:

_____
_____
_____
_____
_____
_____
_____
_____
_____
_____
_____
_____
_____
_____
_____
_____
_____
_____
_____
_____
_____
_____
_____
_____
_____

May

In search of
my mother's garden,
I found my own.

• •

ALICE WALKER

What toys did you like to play with? Why those particular toys?

_____

_____

_____

_____

_____

_____

_____

_____

_____

_____

_____

_____

_____

_____

_____

_____

_____

_____

_____

_____

_____

_____

_____

_____

How old were you when you understood that God loves you?
Recall your early thoughts about God's love.

_____
_____
_____
_____
_____
_____
_____
_____
_____
_____
_____
_____
_____
_____
_____
_____
_____
_____
_____
_____
_____
_____
_____
_____

MAY

*D*escribe a time in your life when you feel God led you in an unusual way.

_____
_____
_____
_____
_____
_____
_____
_____
_____
_____
_____
_____
_____
_____
_____
_____
_____
_____
_____
_____
_____
_____
_____
_____
_____
_____

Did you ever go to a dance? Tell me about it.

What kind of car did your family drive? Were you proud of it or embarrassed by it? Why?

_____

_____

_____

_____

_____

_____

_____

_____

_____

_____

_____

_____

_____

_____

_____

_____

_____

_____

_____

_____

_____

_____

_____

*D*id you attend family reunions?
Share a memory of one.

_____

_____

_____

_____

_____

_____

_____

_____

_____

_____

_____

_____

_____

_____

_____

_____

_____

_____

_____

_____

_____

_____

_____

_____

$\mathcal{D}$id you go to church or community potlucks?
How were they important to you and your family?

$\mathcal{T}$ ell about someone who influenced your life profoundly.

here did you go to grade school? Junior high?
High school? Tell me about your best childhood friend.

_____

_____

_____

_____

_____

_____

_____

_____

_____

_____

_____

_____

_____

_____

_____

_____

_____

_____

_____

_____

_____

_____

_____

If you went to college or to a career training school, where did you go and why?

_____
_____
_____
_____
_____
_____
_____
_____
_____
_____
_____
_____
_____
_____
_____
_____
_____
_____
_____
_____
_____
_____
_____

_W_here did you live when you were going to college or developing a career? Describe an unforgettable experience from that time in your life.

What were your youthful goals and ambitions for life? Which ones have you been able to fulfill?

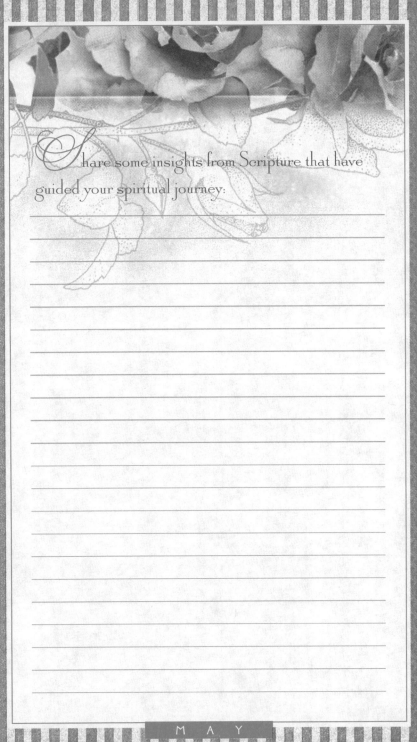

Share some insights from Scripture that have guided your spiritual journey:

_____

_____

_____

_____

_____

_____

_____

_____

_____

_____

_____

_____

_____

_____

_____

_____

_____

_____

_____

_____

_____

_____

MAY

June

Rings and jewels
are not gifts,
but apologies for gifts.
The only gift
is a portion of thyself.

• • •

RALPH WALDO EMERSON

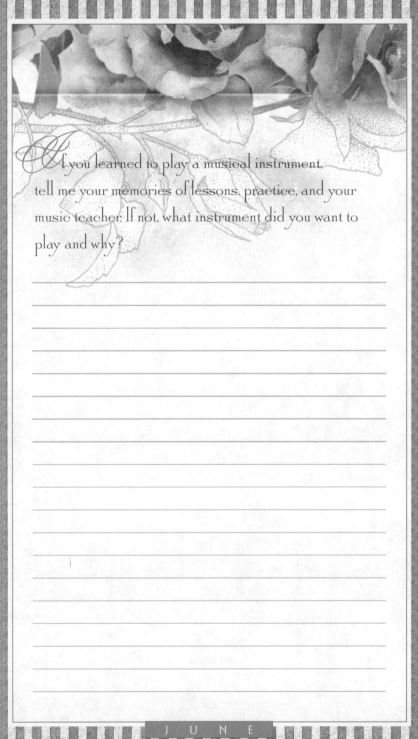

If you learned to play a musical instrument, tell me your memories of lessons, practice, and your music teacher. If not, what instrument did you want to play and why?

What fashions were popular when you were in high school? Did you like them? Why or why not?

*H*ow old were you when you met Dad and what attracted you to him?

_____

_____

_____

_____

_____

_____

_____

_____

_____

_____

_____

_____

_____

_____

_____

_____

_____

_____

_____

_____

_____

_____

*W*hen did you first know you wanted to marry him?
What made you feel that way?

_____

_____

_____

_____

_____

_____

_____

_____

_____

_____

_____

_____

_____

_____

_____

_____

_____

_____

_____

_____

_____

Share a memory about the way he proposed to you.

*W*hat did you wear on your wedding day?

_____

_____

_____

_____

_____

_____

_____

_____

_____

_____

_____

_____

_____

_____

_____

_____

_____

_____

_____

_____

_____

_____

$\mathcal{T}$ell me about your wedding day, from beginning to end.

$\mathcal{D}$id your wedding ceremony include a special vow to each other? What was the significance of it?

*W*here did you go on your honeymoon?
Share one humorous incident.

*W*hat was your first house or apartment together like?

*D*o you remember one of the meals you fixed after you were married? How has your cooking changed since then?

_____

_____

_____

_____

_____

_____

_____

_____

_____

_____

_____

_____

_____

_____

_____

_____

_____

_____

_____

_____

_____

What do you love best about Dad now?

Record here some travel tips or suggestions for a fun-filled vacation:

_____

_____

_____

_____

_____

_____

_____

_____

_____

_____

_____

_____

_____

_____

_____

_____

_____

_____

_____

_____

_____

_____

_____

_____

_____

J U N E

July

I look back and see how
I've become who I am by a family
that found sweetness and joy
somewhere inside when ...
life experience tasted bitter.

KATHY BOICE

Share a family tradition or memory from the Fourth of July.

*H*ave you ever participated in a rally or demonstration? What was the cause? What were your feelings about it?

_W_ho in your family served in the military and when?
Do you have a special memory of that person?

$\mathcal{D}$id you learn to swim? How?

*D*id you ever go camping with your family? Where? Record one exceptional camping experience.

_____
_____
_____
_____
_____
_____
_____
_____
_____
_____
_____
_____
_____
_____
_____
_____
_____
_____
_____
_____
_____
_____
_____

*T*ell about your most memorable
trip by plane, train, or ship.

_____

_____

_____

_____

_____

_____

_____

_____

_____

_____

_____

_____

_____

_____

_____

_____

_____

_____

_____

_____

_____

_____

_____

*D*id you ever travel abroad? How old were you and where did you go? Did you travel alone or with a group?

Describe the most fascinating place you have visited.

Tell about a driving trip with your family.

*D*id your relatives come to visit in the summer or did
you go to visit them? What are your memories of those visits?

*H*ow did you learn to drive? What was your first car like?

id a tragedy ever strike your family? How were you affected?

Share a favorite poem or a passage of writing that has been especially meaningful in your life:

August

The family—that dear
octopus from whose tentacles
we never quite escape,
nor, in our inmost hearts,
ever quite wish to.

DODIE SMITH

ame a book or author that helped you develop
a philosophy of life. Share some of those insights.

Did you have a collection when you were growing up? What initially sparked your interest in it?

Describe a perfect summer day.

What kind of outdoor work do you like? Hate? Why?

If you could be a patron of a charity or organization, which one would you choose? Why?

When did you learn how to ride a bike, or to water ski, snow ski, roller skate, or sail? Share your memories of the experience.

What summer games and activities did your family enjoy?

$\mathcal{D}$id you ever milk a cow or spend time on a farm or in the country? Tell me about it.

Describe your first trip alone.

*W*hat places would you still like to visit? Why?

Describe a frightening or difficult experience from childhood. How did you respond to it?

*T*ell me about your most unforgettable summer experience as a child.

_____

_____

_____

_____

_____

_____

_____

_____

_____

_____

_____

_____

_____

_____

_____

_____

_____

_____

_____

_____

Share some of your ideas about successful
entertaining:

_____

_____

_____

_____

_____

_____

_____

_____

_____

_____

_____

_____

_____

_____

_____

_____

_____

_____

_____

_____

_____

_____

AUGUST

September

Our lives are a mosaic
of little things,
like putting a rose in a
vase on the table.

• • •

INGRID TROBISCH

Did you learn to sew or make other crafts?
How and when? What was the first thing you made?

*T*ell about a special outing you took with your mother or your father.

*W*hat was the most tender day in your childhood?

What was your favorite subject in grade school, junior high, and high school? What was your major in college? Why?

_____
_____
_____
_____
_____
_____
_____
_____
_____
_____
_____
_____
_____
_____
_____
_____
_____
_____
_____
_____
_____
_____
_____
_____
_____

*A*s a young person did you volunteer for work in church, community, or social services? Tell me about it.

When did you move away from home? Describe where you lived and how you felt about it.

Who was your best friend after you were married?
Describe some of the fun things you did together.

*W*hat are your spiritual strengths?

*H*ow would you like to grow spiritually?

_____
_____
_____
_____
_____
_____
_____
_____
_____
_____
_____
_____
_____
_____
_____
_____
_____
_____
_____
_____
_____
_____
_____
_____
_____
_____

What special talents did your parents nurture in you? How have you developed those talents?

What would you like to learn to do? Why?

*W*hat would you do differently in life if you could?

_____
_____
_____
_____
_____
_____
_____
_____
_____
_____
_____
_____
_____
_____
_____
_____
_____
_____
_____
_____
_____

$\mathcal{D}$escribe your personal style in clothing, make up or skin care, and hair care:

_____

_____

_____

_____

_____

_____

_____

_____

_____

_____

_____

_____

_____

_____

_____

_____

_____

_____

_____

_____

_____

_____

_____

October

"How will our children
know who they are
if they don't know
where they came from?"

• • •

MA IN _GRAPES OF WRATH_

*W*ho are some of the best speakers you have ever heard? Why?

_____

_____

_____

_____

_____

_____

_____

_____

_____

_____

_____

_____

_____

_____

_____

_____

_____

_____

_____

_____

_____

_____

_____

_____

What spiritual legacy would you like to leave for others? Why is this important to you?

OCTOBER

*T*ell about a canning or harvesting experience.

What Bible verse or Scripture puzzles you the most? Which blesses you the most? Why?

_____

_____

_____

_____

_____

_____

_____

_____

_____

_____

_____

_____

_____

_____

_____

_____

_____

_____

_____

_____

_____

*H*ave you ever been in an accident, had surgery or a long illness? Tell me about it.

_____
_____
_____
_____
_____
_____
_____
_____
_____
_____
_____
_____
_____
_____
_____
_____
_____
_____
_____
_____
_____
_____
_____
_____
_____

What responsibilities did your parents require of you as a child? Explain how this affected your growth and develpment.

_____

_____

_____

_____

_____

_____

_____

_____

_____

_____

_____

_____

_____

_____

_____

_____

_____

_____

_____

_____

_____

_____

*N*ame your favorite hobby. When and where did you start doing it? Why do you enjoy it?

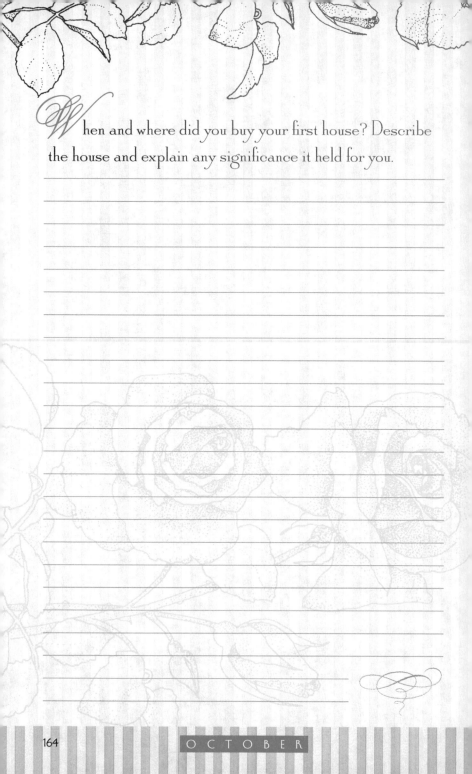

When and where did you buy your first house? Describe the house and explain any significance it held for you.

_____
_____
_____
_____
_____
_____
_____
_____
_____
_____
_____
_____
_____
_____
_____
_____
_____
_____
_____
_____
_____
_____

What is the strangest thing you have ever seen?

Tell about a memorable hotel or resort you have visited.
Describe the location and tell about experiences that were
significant.

*D*id you ever go on a hayride or bob for apples? Tell about fun harvest activities you enjoyed with other young people.

As a teenager, did you belong to a club or church youth group? Tell me about the individuals in the group who were most significant to you.

_____
_____
_____
_____

_____
_____
_____
_____
_____
_____
_____
_____
_____
_____
_____
_____
_____
_____
_____
_____

$\mathcal{S}$hare some helpful home remedies or tips
for good health:

_____

_____

_____

_____

_____

_____

_____

_____

_____

_____

_____

_____

_____

_____

_____

_____

_____

_____

_____

_____

_____

_____

November

In our family an experience
was not finished,
nor truly experienced,
unless written down or
shared with another.

• • •

ANNE MORROW LINDBERGH

What individuals have had the greatest impact
on your spiritual life? How did they impact your life?

_____

_____

_____

_____

_____

_____

_____

_____

_____

_____

_____

_____

_____

_____

_____

_____

_____

_____

_____

_____

_____

_____

_____

_____

NOVEMBER

What is your most treasured possession and why?

What Bible character would you most like to meet? Why?

*W*hat is your most vivid memory of being pregnant?

How ow did you choose my name and why?

_____
_____
_____
_____
_____
_____
_____
_____
_____
_____
_____
_____
_____
_____
_____
_____
_____
_____
_____
_____
_____
_____
_____

*W*hat is your most poignant
memory about my childhood?

_____

_____

_____

_____

_____

_____

_____

_____

_____

_____

_____

_____

_____

_____

_____

_____

_____

_____

_____

_____

_____

_____

_____

_____

_____

_____

*W*hat was a favorite Thanksgiving tradition in your family?

What are some things from your childhood that you are thankful for?

What childhood memory first comes to mind when you think about winter? How do you respond to that memory?

_____

_____

_____

_____

_____

_____

_____

_____

_____

_____

_____

_____

_____

_____

_____

_____

_____

_____

_____

_____

_____

_____

_____

_____

_____

_____

*W*hat are your childhood memories of going to church or of interacting with other Christians?

What family custom would you like to pass on to your children and grandchildren?

_____

_____

_____

_____

_____

_____

_____

_____

_____

_____

_____

_____

_____

_____

_____

_____

_____

_____

_____

_____

_____

_____

_____

_____

_____

_____

*W*hat new tradition would you like to start in the family? What is its significance?

_____
_____
_____
_____
_____
_____
_____
_____
_____
_____
_____
_____
_____
_____
_____
_____
_____
_____
_____
_____
_____
_____

Share a favorite Thanksgiving or Christmas recipe.

December

If everything special and warm
and happy in my formative years
could have been consolidated
into one word, that word
would have been *Christmas*.

• • •

GLORIA GAITHER

Tell about some Christmas rituals in your family and how you felt about them.

Were you ever in a Christmas program? How did you respond to the experience?

What favorite Christmas treasures have you kept from year to year? Share their origins.

$\mathscr{T}$ell about a memorable Christmas visit with relatives.

What is your favorite Christmas carol? Why?

$\mathcal{D}$id you have a Christmas
stocking as a child or a special
ornament? What did it look like?

$\mathcal{D}$escribe the Christmas that has been the most meaningful to you.

What would be the most wonderful gift you could receive? Why?

_____
_____
_____
_____
_____
_____
_____
_____
_____
_____
_____
_____
_____
_____
_____
_____
_____
_____
_____
_____
_____
_____
_____

Tell me about a time when God answered a specific prayer for you.

_____

_____

_____

_____

_____

_____

_____

_____

_____

_____

_____

_____

_____

_____

_____

_____

_____

_____

_____

_____

_____

_____

_____

What would you like to see happen in the next ten years?

*W*hat has been the happiest time of your life?

What word best describes your life? Explain why.

What advice about life do you want others to remember?

_____

_____

_____

_____

_____

_____

_____

_____

_____

_____

_____

_____

_____

_____

_____

_____

_____

_____

_____

_____

_____

_____

NOTES

NOTES

NOTES

PHOTOS

PHOTOS

PHOTOS